MOCY PUBLISHING

Copyright © 2017 Mocy Publishing, LLC
All rights reserved. Printed in the U.S.A.

Printed by CreateSpace, An Amazon.com Company

What Would Lil' Jesus Do?
ISBN 978-1-940831-36-7
Copyright © 2017 by Alicia White & Victor Walker
Illustrator: James Gullat

Royal Tykes Children's Book
Published by Mocy Publishing, LLC.
Website: www.mocypublishing.com
Email: info@mocypublishing.com

All rights reserved. Except as permitted under the United States Copyright Act of 1976, no part of this publication may be reproduced or distributed in any form or by any means, or stored in a data base or retrieval system, without the prior written permission of the publisher.

WHAT WOULD LIL' JESUS DO?

"...and how from infancy you have known the Holy Scriptures, which are able to make you wise for salvation through faith in Christ Jesus. ALL Scriptures is GOD-breathed and is useful for teaching, rebuking, correcting and training in righteousness, so that the servant of GOD may be thoroughly equipped for every good work."

-2 Timothy 3:15-17

Once upon a time, in a small neighborhood, there lived a mean, little boy named Jacob. He was eight years old with a scar on his face and had a really bad attitude. - (Proverbs 14:10; 29:22).

One hot, summer day he was standing outside with a can of blue spray paint. He had just finished writing on his neighbor's garage when another little boy walked over. - (1 Corinthians 15:33; Proverbs 2:11).

"Hi, my name is Lil' Jesus," said the young boy. "What's your name?" Jacob turned around swiftly. "My name is Jacob," he said, "but some people call me Jac. I'm the toughest eight year old in the whole neighborhood!" - (Proverbs 16-5; 21:24; Galatians 6:3). "You wanna go with me to tag some more walls?" - (Proverbs 4:14-15; 5:22; 15:26).

"Oh no!," said Lil' Jesus. "I was just walking through the neighborhood and I saw you standing out here, so I stop to say, Hello." - (Luke 19:10; 24:15-16). "Is that so?," asked Jacob. "Well, I guess I'll just head back toward my house with you then." - (Proverbs 4:26-27).

As both boys, quietly walked home together, Jacob waved to Lil' Jesus and said he would see Him again tomorrow. Lil' Jesus didn't respond, He just stopped walking and folded His arms. - (Proverbs 4:14-15; 10:9).

The next day, Jac woke up early in the morning, snuck into his mother's bedroom and stole some money out of her purse. - (Exodus 20:12, 15; Proverbs 28:24). His plan was to go outside, meet with Lil' Jesus, then buy something from the candy store...

But by the time he opened his front door, Lil' Jesus had already passed by and was walking toward the school yard. - (Exodus 33:19; 1 Kings 19:11). "Hey Lil' Jesus... Wait up!," said Jacob.

Minutes later, both boys walked into the candy store and Jac began buying up everything! He had so much stuff in his shopping bag that he could barely hold it all. - (Proverbs 28:25). "Where did you get money for all of this candy?," asked Lil' Jesus. But Jac, quickly, made up a story saying that his mother gave it to him. - (Proverbs 12:22; 19:5).

Suddenly, Jac, swiftly, took off running and dropped his snacks to the ground. He had just saw a little boy parking his car playing with a new computer. - (Exodus 20:17; Proverbs 14:17).

Jacob then pulled out his slingshot and slugged the kid with a rock. - (Proverbs 18:1; 21:7). "Take that!," he said. "This is my neighborhood, fool!" - (Proverbs 6:12-15; 17:20).

The little boy wept, with tears in his eyes, as Jac took his favorite belongings. He even kneeled on the roadside, begging for help, but Jacob was already gone. - (Proverbs 6:16-19; 21:10).

Later that day, Jac met Lil' Jesus as He fixed His wooden go cart. "What are you doing, Lil' Jesus?," asked Jacob. Lil' Jesus didn't answer him, He just continued working quietly.

- (Proverbs 12:14, 26; 14:22).

Jac then pulled out his stolen Lap top to watch an adult movie. - (1 Thessalonsians 4:2-5,). Lil' Jesus just stared at him. "I'm really disappointed in you, Jacob!, " He said. "You are not behaving like a good eight year old boy!." - (Proverbs 16:23; 17:17; 18:21).

"Aw, Lighten up!," said Jacob. "ALL I'm trying to do is have a little fun." - (Proverbs 10:23; 14:13). Lil' Jesus then walked over and stood next to him... - (Proverbs 15:23).

"My Father says, you should always do unto others as you want them to do unto you. - (Luke 6:31). But you haven't been doing that, and I am very ashamed of you!," He said. - (Proverbs 12:15). "My Father also says, whatever you think in your heart is who you really are. - (Proverbs 23:7 KJV), so you should always think about things that are true, honest and good. - (Philippians 4:8).

"That sounds stupid!," said Jacob. But he was so embarrassed that he really didn't know what else to say. - (Proverbs 12:1; 14:3). "If you really want to be my friend," said Lil' Jesus, "then you're gonna have to stop all that bad behavior. - (Proverbs 22:24). I really want us to be buddies, but you just keep causing trouble. - (Proverbs 12:26; 13:21). So, now, you have to make a choice." - (Acts 3:19 -20).

Jacob then dropped his head down and started crying. - (Proverbs 14:19). "I know that I've done some bad things, Lil' Jesus, and I'm sorry! - (1 John 1:9); I really do want to change!," said Jacob. "But I've been being bad for so long now, I don't even know how to be good any more." - (Romans 3: 23 -24; Isaiah 40:29 -31; 53:6). He felt so ashamed of himself.

"Sure you do!," said Lil' Jesus. "All you have to do is Believe. - (John 11:25 -26, 40), Repent - (Matthew 4:17) and accept Me as your Best Friend - (Psalms 54:6), and all of your bad behavior will disappear." - (2 Corinthians 5:17). Jacob then lifted his head up, wiping away his tears and ask, "Really, Lil' Jesus?!" "Sure will," He said. "You can do it all by yourself!" - (Luke 17:21; Philippians 2:13; 1 John 4:4).

Jac finally decided to accept Lil' Jesus as his friend. And they agreed to be buddies forever and ever. "Someday," said Lil' Jesus, Jac would receive everything that he wants from His Father. - (Matthew 6:33; 7:7 -8). Lil' Jesus also gave Jacob one of His favorite books to read - it was called, The Holy Bible. - (Psalms 19:7-11; 119:9; 1 Peter 2:2 -3).

Three days later, both boys returned each thing that Jac had stolen from other people - the money, the car, and the lap top computer. - (Psalms 51:10; Matthew 5:9). "I'm really glad you chose to be my friend!," said Lil' Jesus. "So am I?" said Jacob. "After all, everyone needs a Lil' Jesus in their life!" "Amen!," said Lil' Jesus.

THE END

STUDY REFERENCES

ANXIETY & ASSURANCE
Psalms 37: 1-5
Proverbs 16:3
Isaiah 41:10
John 5:24; 20:31
Romans 8:16, 31
Philippians 4:6 -9
Hebrew 13:5
1 Peter 5:5-7
1 John 5:11 -13

COMFORT & CONFIDENCE
Psalms 23
Proverbs 14:26
Matthew 11:28 – 30
John 14:18, 27
2 Corinthians 1:3-5
2 Peter 3:9

DANGER & DIFFICULTY
Psalms 34:17; 9:11; 121:7-8
Romans 14:8
2 Corinthians 4:6 -9, 17

FEAR/FAITH/FORGIVENESS
Psalms 27:1; 56:11; 121:8
Proverbs 3:25; 28:13
Isaiah 55:7
Luke 12:22 -32
Hebrews 11:1
James 2:20; 5:15-16
1 John 1:9

FRIENDS
Proverbs 18:24
John 15:13-14

GOD & GOODNESS
Psalms 37:3
Matthew 18:20
Luke 17:21
John 1:1-4; 14:6-7, 20
Philippians 2:6
Hebrews 13:8
1 John 4:4

HONESTY & HUMANITY
Exodus 20:16
John 8:32
Micah 6:8
Romans 12:3
Philippians 4:8
Thessalonians 4:11-12
Hebrews 13:16
1 Peter 2:11; 5:5-6

LOVE
John 3:16; 14:21; 15:9-14
Galatians 5:14
1 John 3:1

MORALS
Luke 6:31
Galatians 6:7-8
Ephesians 5:3-7

OBEDIENCE
Psalms 119:1-2
Ecclesiastes 12:13
2 Corinthians 10:5
1 John 3:22

PARENTS & CHILDREN
Exodus 20:12, 15
Proverbs 1:8 -9; 6:20 -23; 22:6
Mark 10:13-16
Ephesians 6:1-4
Colossians 3:20-21
1 Timothy 4:12

PRAYER & PEACE
Psalms 18:1-3; 34:14; 86:5, 7; 145:14-19
Jeremiah 33:3
Matthew 5:9; 6:9-15; 7:7-8; 21-22
John 14:13-14
Philippians 4:9
James 5:16
1 John 5:14-15

REWARDS
Ephesians 6:8
2 Thessalonians 2:14
2 Timothy 4:8
James 1:17

SALVATION
John 5:24; 10:9-10
Acts 4:11 – 12
Romans 8:1-2
Galatians 5:1
Ephesians 6:13-18
Colossians 2:6
1 John 5:11-12

SIN
Matthew 18:21
John 8:34
Romans 3:23; 6:23; 12:2
1 Corinthians 15-33
Galatians 6:7 -8

SORROW
Matthew 11:28 -30; 26:38
John 16:22
2 Corinthians 1:3 -5; 4:17 -18
Revelations 21:4

STRENGTH
Psalms 26:7 -8
Isaiah 40:29 -31
2 Corinthians 12:9
Philippians 4:13
Ephesians 3:16-17

TEMPTATION
Psalms 94:17 -18
Proverbs 28:13
Isaiah 41:10
1 Corinthians 10:12-13
Philippians 4:14 -16
2 Thessalonians 3:3
James 4:7
1 Peter 2:9

TEN COMMANDMENTS
Exodus 20:1-17

VICTORY

Romans 8:37

1 Corinthians 15:57

2 Corinthians 2:14

1 John 5:4

Revelations 3:5; 21:7

WILL OF GOD

Psalms 37:4

Proverbs 3:5 -6; 4:20 -27; 14:5

Galatians 6:4

Ephesians 5:14 -17

Philippians 2:12 -13

1 Thessalonians 4:3

1 Peter 3:17

WISDOM

Proverbs 23:7 (KJV)

The Rayion Myatt K.I.N.D. KIDS Fundraiser Program is a local charity-based initiative, specifically, established to benefit single mothers and their children in need of supplemental/paternal support.

Founded in 2015, by educator, Alicia White and her six year old son, Rayion Myatt, the K.I.N.D. KIDS program is a collective effort on their behalf to assist as many underprivileged families as they possibly can reach.

The K.I.N.D. KIDS acronym simply stands for **Kids In Need of a Dad**. And the primary purpose of this program is to help make a positive difference in the beautiful lives of single mothers and their children.

For more information, please visit:
www.facebook.com/The Rayion Myatt K.I.N.D. KIDS Fundraiser Program
and www.zazzle.com/The KIND KIDS STORE

A portion of all proceeds derived from sales of this children's book will be donated to local charities and underprivileged residents on behalf of The Rayion Myatt K.I.N.D. KIDS Fundraiser Program.